The Civil War

Moments in History

by Shirley Jordan

Perfection Learning® CA

About the Author

Shirley Jordan is a retired elementary school teacher and principal. Currently a lecturer in the teacher-training program at California State University, Fullerton, California, she sees exciting things happening in the world of social studies. Shirley loves to travel—with a preference for sites important to U.S. history.

She has had more than 50 travel articles published in recent years. It was through her travels that she became interested in "moments in history," those ironic and little-known stories that make one exclaim, "I didn't know that!" Such stories are woven throughout her books.

Image Credits: Art Today cover map, pp. 3, 4 bottom, 6 top, 10 bottom, 13, 21 bottom, 22, 24, 26 top, 27 top, 41 bottom, 42, 51 bottom; Library of Congress cover photos back and front, pp. 4 top, 4 third, 5, 6 bottom, 7 top, 8 bottom, 9, 11, 14 bottom, 16, 18, 19, 20 top, 21 top, 25, 26 middle and bottom, 27 middle and bottom, 28 second third and bottom, 29 bottom, 35, 36, 37, 38, 39, 40, 41 top, 44 top, 45, 46, 47, 50, 51 top, 53 bottom, 54, 56; National Archives pp. 4 second, 8 top, 10 top, 14 top, 17, 20 bottom, 27 top, 29 top, 31, 32, 43, 44 bottom, 49, 53 top.

Printed in the United States of America. For information, contact
Perfection Learning® Corporation,
1000 North Second Avenue, P.O. Box 500,
Logan, Iowa 51546.
Phone: 1-800-831-4190 • Fax: 1-712-644-2392
Paperback ISBN 0-7891-2903-5
Cover Craft® ISBN 0-7807-8049-3

Table of Contents

A Timeline of Important Events

**1830–
1860**   Slaves begin to escape from the Southern states.

1860   Abraham Lincoln is elected president of the
United States.

South Carolina leaves, or *secedes* from,
the Union. Six other states follow.

1861   Southern troops attack Fort Sumter in
Charleston, South Carolina.

Four more states leave the Union.

Richmond, Virginia, is chosen as the
Confederate capital.

Confederate troops win the Battle of Bull Run.

1862   Union troops win the Battle of Shiloh. Thousands of men
from both sides are killed.

The *Monitor* and the *Merrimac*
warships meet in battle.

1862   Union ships take New Orleans, Louisiana.

General Robert E. Lee's Confederate army stops the North's drive toward Richmond.

The Confederate army drafts men to fill its ranks.

1863   President Lincoln signs the Emancipation Proclamation.

The North begins to draft men for military service.

After three days of bitter fighting, the North turns back the Confederate troops at Gettysburg.

1864   General Ulysses S. Grant leads the Union army's second attack on Richmond.

Union General William T. Sherman marches from Tennessee to Georgia. His troops destroy everything of value to the South.

Abraham Lincoln is reelected.

1865   The Confederates abandon their capital.

General Lee surrenders to General Grant.

The 13th Amendment ends slavery in the United States.

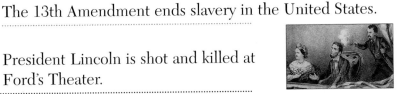

President Lincoln is shot and killed at Ford's Theater.

Chapter 1

A Nation Divided

In the 1850s, most Southerners were farmers. It took many workers to farm the land. And slave labor was used. Most Northerners worked in factories and lived in cities. And they were against slavery. A great debate over this issue went on in Congress.

Meanwhile, slaves risked their lives to escape from the Southern farms, or *plantations.* They hoped to reach the nearest free state. For example, slaves from Kentucky ran to Ohio. And those from Maryland ran away to Pennsylvania.

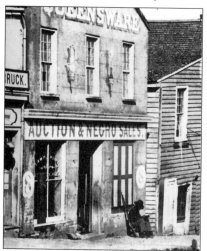

These runaways were seeking freedom. And Northern citizens who hated slavery were willing to help them.

But not all families in the North were against slavery. And not all those in the South approved of it. In many families, brothers and sisters argued among themselves about it. Neighbors even became enemies over it.

States that were close to the line between North and South were the *border states*, for example, Kentucky, Tennessee, and Virginia. Families in border states were often split by their beliefs. Sometimes one brother might join the Union forces, while another brother joined the Confederate forces.

President Abraham Lincoln's wife knew such a division in her own family. During the Civil War, Mary Todd Lincoln supported the Union cause. But her younger brother, David H. Todd, served as an officer in the Confederacy.

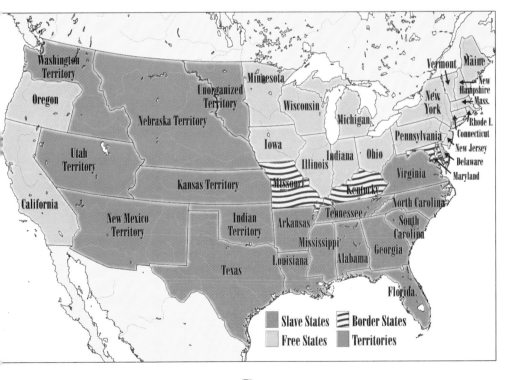

Chapter 2

Daring Escapes

One-Way Ticket on the Underground Railroad

By the early 1860s, increasing numbers of slaves were escaping to the North. The journey was dangerous. But life as a slave was so bitter that most were willing to take a chance.

Let's join Ben, a 14-year-old slave. He and his family are preparing to escape. They would travel on the Underground Railroad.

"When are we leaving?" asked Ben. "Isn't everybody here?"

He looked around the small cabin. He'd grown up there. It was dark. Just a few coals were glowing in the fireplace.

Papa, Mama, Ben's sister Minnie, and his Aunt Bess were with him.

His cousins John, 14, and Sam, 15, sat on the dirt floor. Between them were cloth bundles of corn cakes and salted herring. There was enough food for two days of walking.

"Whisper, Ben," his mother said softly. "We don't know who might tell on us. There might be bounty hunters listening at the window.

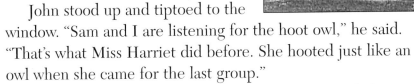

"If they see us leaving, they'll sound the alarm for sure. Turning us in means a lot of money for them."

John stood up and tiptoed to the window. "Sam and I are listening for the hoot owl," he said. "That's what Miss Harriet did before. She hooted just like an owl when she came for the last group."

Ben was careful to keep his voice low. "I've heard about someone called Moses," he said. "But who is Miss Harriet?"

"It's the same person, son," whispered Papa. He put his hand on his worn Bible.

"Harriet Tubman is like Moses in the good book. She leads her people out of slavery. That's why folks call her that."

From outside came the soft sounds of a single voice. Snatches of a hymn came to them.

"Go down, Moses. Way down to Egypt land."

Papa reached for Minnie's hand. Then he reached for Ben's.

"There," he said softly. "That's the signal. Moses has come. She's here."

Ben felt a shiver go through his body. His sister, still quiet, wiped away a tear.

The door opened. And a 42-year-old woman slipped into the cabin.

The group was very quiet. Here was Harriet Tubman! The woman who had risked her life to save so many others. Folks said there were signs tacked up in town. The reward for catching Miss Harriet was $40,000!

"You're the answer to our prayers," Mama whispered. "We heard just yesterday—the slave trader is on his way. They mean to take our children away from us and sell them."

Harriet Tubman smiled. "Then we just have to give that old slave trader a surprise, don't we? You can't sell what you can't find."

She touched each of them on the shoulder. She said, "If you got some warmer things, bring them along. We're going all the way to Canada."

Ben didn't know where that was. But he was ready to follow Moses.

Miss Harriet turned to Papa. "I thought you had one more passenger for me," she said.

Everyone was still. At last, Aunt Bess spoke.

"My husband Fred was sold just last week. The owner said he was making trouble. But it wasn't true!"

Moses was thoughtful. "Well, if we can't help him, we'll just have to help his family. I'll take you and your boys to freedom. I promise."

They left the cabin and began to walk along the dark path toward town. They were in the greatest danger near home. They knew that. Someone might recognize them. They wanted to walk 15 miles that first night.

Moses is smart, Ben thought. She came for us on a

Saturday night. On Sundays, not many people are on the roads. We might not be missed until Monday morning. That's when we're supposed to be back in the fields.

All night, the travelers walked along the road. They stayed close to the woods along the side. Twice they heard wagons coming and hid in the trees.

"Sometimes Moses takes folks with small babies," Mama said. "That's dangerous. At least we don't have anyone along that can't be quiet."

They walked and walked. It was the longest and scariest night of Ben's life.

When daylight came, they moved far into the woods. They found places to sleep under the trees.

Miss Harriet cheered them up with tales of her own escape. She told them how she'd thought the Underground Railroad really was a train. She thought it had tracks under the earth. She thought they stretched all the way to the North.

She had run away from Maryland alone.

"I followed the *drinking gourd*," she said. "That's a big group of stars that looks like a gourd. Something you'd use to scoop up drinking water. Follow the brightest two stars with your eye. They point to the North Star."

A smile lit up her face. "I just headed for the North Star. And it took me to freedom."

Ben liked her story. But he was afraid to go to sleep. What if the bounty hunters came? Was there a safe place ahead?

Even after he closed his eyes, Ben heard his father and mother moving around. No one slept well that day.

After another night of walking, the woods felt safer. Sleep came a little easier. They were farther from the plantation and farther from those who would be looking for them.

That night, Miss Harriet told Ben and Minnie more stories. She told about her days as a slave child. She told about the beatings and how little she'd had to eat.

When morning came, it began to rain. But the family slept. Ben simply leaned against a tree and closed his eyes. He was too tired to care about danger.

On the fourth night, they trudged along the road. By now, the corn cakes and smoked fish were gone. Ben was hungry. But Moses promised them a warm place and good food before morning.

She kept talking about reaching a "station." And she called them her "passengers."

She talks like we're on a real railroad, thought Ben.

It was a hard journey. But at least they were closer to freedom!

Just before morning, Moses led them down a narrow path. It was rutted by wagon wheels. Mud squished under Ben's feet. He slid and almost fell.

A large farmhouse stood before them. The runaways hid behind trees while Moses went to the door. When she knocked, a man's voice asked, "Who is it?"

"A friend with friends," Moses said. This was the password of the Underground Railroad.

The door opened and Ben saw a tall, broad-shouldered gentleman. He had a kind face.

"Blessings to thee. All of thee." The door opened wide. Quickly, they scurried inside. They had reached the first station.

Soon they were in a warm, tidy kitchen. Hot food was waiting for them. Ben filled his plate over and over.

This family of Quakers would give them a place to sleep. And they'd help them to the next station.

The Quaker church taught that skin color is not important. That what is in the heart is important. These kind people were willing to risk everything to help slaves escape.

All that day, Ben and his family slept in a large, clean barn. When they awoke, Moses brought good news. The farmer had a wagon big enough for them all.

Mama, Papa, his Aunt Bess, and Moses lay down in the back of the wagon. The four children crowded around them.

Then the Quaker family spread blankets over everybody. On top went farm tools and bundles of hay. As the sun went down, the wagon headed north along the road. There would be no miles to walk that night.

The next day, they slept in the attic of a free black family. Then they walked 10 miles along the dark roads.

Their next stations brought them to a group of Germans, then another Quaker household. At each place, Moses  whispered, "A friend with friends."

Ben wondered why others would take such a risk for them. One day, he asked Papa what would happen if they were caught.

"Well, son," Papa began, "we'd be sent back to the plantation. We'd all be punished—probably whipped. Then you children would be sold. And your mama and I would be sent to another plantation. One deep in the South."

"What about the folks who helped us at the stations?"

His father sighed. "Sometimes they do get caught. When that happens, the judge fines them. They have to pay the same amount their house and farm are worth. They usually have to sell everything they own to pay the fine. Then they're poor forever."

"And Miss Harriet?"

"She'd be hanged, son."

As they walked up the path to their next station, Moses turned to the group. A wide smile spread across her face.

"Dear friends," she said. "Welcome to the North. We're now in Pennsylvania."

Ben felt as though his heart could fly. They had walked 90 miles. And now they were really in a free state—Pennsylvania.

His mother and aunt dropped to their knees to give thanks. The family members hugged each other. Free at last!

Moses raised her hand. "You've still got to be careful," she warned. "I used to bring my passengers this far and leave them. They were safe.

"But since then, the government passed the Fugitive Slave Law. So folks in the North must turn in anyone they think is a runaway. If they don't, they go to jail. You won't be really safe till we get to Canada."

"Will that be soon?" asked Ben.

"I'm afraid not," Moses answered. "It's going to be another 300 miles. But you don't have to walk, young man."

Harriet Tubman's many friends in the North were ready to help. Wagons were rented. Food was bought for the trip. Ben's family had warm new clothes and strong shoes.

But the winter weather bothered the travelers. The family wasn't used to such cold.

CAUTION!!
COLORED PEOPLE
OF BOSTON, ONE & ALL,

You are hereby respectfully CAUTIONED and advised, to avoid conversing with the

Watchmen and Police Officers of Boston,

For since the recent ORDER OF THE MAYOR & ALDERMEN, they are empowered to act as

KIDNAPPERS
AND
Slave Catchers,

And they have already been actually employed in KIDNAPPING, CATCHING, AND KEEPING SLAVES. Therefore, if you value your LIBERTY, and the *Welfare of the Fugitives* among you, *Shun* them in every possible manner, as so many *HOUNDS* on the track of the most unfortunate of your race.

Keep a Sharp Look Out for KIDNAPPERS, and have TOP EYE open.
APRIL 24, 1851.

On they went, through New Jersey and into New York. There they were given train tickets.

Ben liked it when they sat in fine, clean train seats. But when Moses thought they might be in danger, they rode in the baggage car.

In Rochester, they stayed in the home of Frederick Douglass. He was a former slave. He was famous for his own brave escape and for his work to free his people.

Once in Canada, Harriet Tubman rented a small house. She and the group moved in. It was too late in the year for her to make another trip to Maryland.

Everyone set out to find work of any kind. They did housework. They chopped wood. And they did hauling and repairing. Many people in town knew Moses. They found jobs for her friends.

Ben looked around him. He missed the gentle weather of Maryland. He missed the streams and the swamps. He missed his friends.

But he didn't miss being a slave. Here he was free!

This Train Is Heading North

Here are three more stories of slaves who escaped to the North. These men and women used real railroads. They rode the Philadelphia, Wilmington, and Baltimore Railroad. Their route ran from Baltimore to Philadelphia.

Charlotte Giles and Harriett Eglin

Charlotte Giles and Harriett Eglin were slaves in Maryland. They put on long black dresses and heavy veils. This made them look like *widows* in mourning. (That means women who are grieving because their husbands have died.)

With their faces covered, they bought tickets on the railroad. And the two women escaped to Philadelphia.

Frederick Douglass

Frederick Douglass, a famous black writer and speaker, longed to escape to the North. In his state, Maryland, all free black people had to carry freedom papers with them. The papers proved that they were not slaves.

In 1838, Douglass borrowed the papers of a friend. His friend was a black American sailor. Dressing in uniform, he bought a railroad ticket from Baltimore to Philadelphia.

Douglass was afraid that he would be caught. The conductors kept looking at him and asking questions. But they did not discover that he was a runaway.

Douglass made it safely to the North. And he spent the rest of his life working to free other blacks from slavery.

The Crafts

Runaway slaves William and Ellen Craft escaped by night. They walked from Macon, Georgia, to Baltimore. There they formed a plan to get to the North.

Ellen had very light skin. She dressed as a gentleman. Pretending to be William's owner, she bought two railroad tickets.

She and William were careful not to speak to other passengers on the train. Finally, they reached Philadelphia—and freedom.

Chapter 3

The Family That Couldn't Escape

Wilmer McLean had had enough. Union soldiers in blue uniforms were marching from the North. Confederate troops in gray were coming from the South. His Manassas, Virginia, farm was right between the two groups.

McLean wanted his family to be safe. But how could he keep them from harm?

In town, nobody thought the Civil War would happen. Americans would never fight other Americans!

Well, the news about Fort Sumter was a worry. And President Lincoln had called for men to join the army. But would there be a war? McLean and his friends didn't want to believe it. Couldn't this problem about slavery be settled some other way?

It was the spring of 1861. Seven Southern states had already left the Union. The farmers in those states were angry. They were afraid that President Lincoln would make them free their slaves.

How could they be expected to plant large pieces of land alone? How could a man grow cotton, tobacco, and sugar

without many workers? These things couldn't be done without slaves. The landowners decided to fight to keep things the way they were!

McLean was a Southerner. And Virginia was a slave state. He knew how the planters felt. If it came to a fight, he would surely have to side with his neighbors.

Because McLean lived so far north in Virginia, his home was only 20 miles from Washington, D.C. If fighting came, his farm would be right in the middle of the battle.

Now it looked as if both North and South wanted to control the railroad line in Manassas. Each day, war seemed closer.

More Union forces gathered at Manassas. The railroad line helped move troops and supplies.

Confederate soldiers marched to McLean's farm too. The two armies camped on either side of a winding stream called Bull Run.

For weeks, no shots were fired. Sticky summer heat brought mosquitoes and flies. The insects got into everything. The food was poor. Both armies lived on dried meat and hard bread.

The men slept on bare dirt. When it rained, mud covered the tired soldiers and their weapons.

An outbreak of measles swept through the camps. Even without a war, many soldiers died each week.

Wilmer McLean invited the Confederate officers to move into his farmhouse. The officers asked for a signal tower. And he allowed one to be built in his front yard. He would do all he could to help.

Still, McLean worried about his family's safety.

The rich people of nearby Washington, D.C., didn't worry at all. "A battle down at Manassas would end the war," they said.

The first shots rang out on July 21, 1861.

The people of Washington dressed for an outing. They piled their children into family wagons. Then they added baskets of food. They added some blankets to sit on. They rode 20 miles down the road to Manassas.

"This is just like a picnic," some said. "How exciting! A chance to see a real battle!"

But what happened wasn't a game. The Confederate army rushed forward. They forced the Union soldiers backward, toward Washington.

Many soldiers were wounded. As bloody bodies filled the road, the picnic crowd panicked. They rushed back to the city in terror.

The battle shocked Wilmer McLean too. A large cannon shell burst through his kitchen window. And before the fighting stopped, wounded Confederate soldiers filled his house. Instead of a headquarters, his house had turned into a hospital.

McLean was glad that the South had won that day. But his heart was heavy as he looked around him. His home was damaged. His fields were trampled. His fences were down. All his crops had been torn up or destroyed.

No one in his own family was hurt. But McLean knew how close the danger had come. He gathered his loved ones at the end of the day.

"This will not happen again," he said firmly. "I promise you. I will take you far from here to the Virginia hill country. We will start over there. The war will never reach us."

And he kept his promise. He found a small village. It was more than a hundred miles south of Manassas. It was far from the railroad line. No army would have reason to come there.

The McLeans built a two-story brick house. It had a wide porch and a fine set of front steps.

From the porch, the family could see the town square and the brick tavern. A new courthouse stood nearby. Because of that, the village was named Appomattox Courthouse.

The Civil War lasted for four more years. But McLean felt safe for most of that time.

Then in 1865, the Union troops won battle after battle. They pushed the Confederate soldiers farther into the South.

Again, the McLeans could hear the sounds of war. The family gathered.

McLean said, "We must pray the fighting won't find us again."

On April 9, 1865, a tired Confederate colonel came down the street. He looked around. Then he climbed the stairs to the McLeans' wide porch.

The colonel had a question. You see, General Robert E. Lee and the Confederates were ready to give up. There would be no more war. No more blood would flow.

But Lee needed a place to *surrender,* or give up the fight. He and the Union General Ulysses S. Grant had to work out the peace plans.

The colonel asked, "Would you allow your parlor to be used for the meeting?"

Wilmer McLean was glad to see an end to the fighting. So he agreed. After all, it had all begun in his kitchen in Manassas. Shouldn't it end in his new home?

Chapter 4

Family Life

Life in the North

Imagine that you are living in the North. You are white. And it is 1860...

Your father, like many others, is a factory worker. Cotton grown in the South makes it possible for companies in the North to produce fine woven cloth. Much of this cloth is shipped to Europe.

This arrangement between the South and the North makes money for both. Many people do not want anything changed.

Like most Americans, your family is not rich. But you have enough to eat. And you go to a free, public school.

Around your city, there are small towns and farm country. The people you know there aren't rich either. But life is comfortable.

All the Northern states have freed their slaves. But freedom from slavery does not mean an easy life. The poorest citizens of the North are the

250,000 freed blacks. They have a hard time finding work. There are not enough jobs for everyone. And when there is a job, whites are hired first.

If you were black, you would have no school and no right to vote. You could not sue a white person in court. Your family would be free to go to church, but only with other blacks.

Your parents are talking about the changing times. Their friends have told them about *Uncle Tom's Cabin.* This book about slave life was written by Harriet Beecher Stowe. The book has stirred up readers in the North. They want to know why life is hard for the slaves.

Abraham Lincoln is president. Now the Southern states want to have their own nation. But President Lincoln believes the United States should be held together. Many men in the North agree with him. And they join the army.

The war creates more business for factories and for farms in the North. There is a great need for iron and steel for weapons. And the soldiers need woolen uniforms and shoes. Farmers are busy growing crops to feed the troops.

Sometimes you wave flags. And you sing songs to cheer the soldiers on.

Life in the South

Now imagine that you are living in the South. You are white. And it is 1860...

You live on farmland—like most other kids. The country is warm. And crops grow well. All around are huge fields of cotton, rice, and tobacco. The nearest city is miles and miles away.

A few families live in huge plantation houses. They wear fine clothes. Their children go to expensive schools. These families shape life in the South.

There are about 3,000 slave owners in the South. A rich owner might own 200 slaves. Some slaves work in the house. They cook and clean. But most slaves work in the fields all day.

Your family is poor, however. This is common. Your father goes from farm to farm trying to find work. There are no slaves in your house.

Sometimes your parents hire one from a nearby plantation. They hire a slave just on days when there is extra work to be done. That slave's pay goes directly to his owner.

You might hear your parents talking about *states' rights.* Many think the Southern states should have a country of their own. That way, Congress can't force them to end slavery.

Southerners want slavery to continue. Even poor whites want this. People think that there wouldn't be enough paying jobs for everyone if slaves were freed.

"This arguing might turn into a war between the states," your parents say. "But if it does, England might help the South in the fight. They want to buy our cotton."

If you were black in the South, someone would own you. That person would be known as your *master.*

You could be sold away from your parents. Sometimes you might be hired out to another white master. You could be willed to the sons and daughters of your master. You could even be lost to another player in a card game.

A few free blacks might live in the countryside with you. They would have earned or been given freedom by a kind master. Sometimes this happens when a master with no children dies.

For freed slaves, life is still hard. The law doesn't allow them to own land or keep a gun, not even for hunting meat. Free blacks cannot meet with slaves.

Southerners are being arrested for owning a copy of *Uncle Tom's Cabin.* That book tells too many secrets about slave life.

One black man was sentenced to ten years in prison just for reading the book!

Even so, readers—both black and white—rush to find copies of that book.

Chapter 5

Civil War Leaders

Confederate Leaders

General Robert E. Lee was one of the most respected men of his time. He was known for his honesty and sense of duty.

Unlike most Southerners, Lee did not believe in slavery. He did not want to see the nation divided. Lincoln offered him command of the Union troops. But Lee decided to remain loyal to his home state of Virginia.

In May 1861, he was made a full general in the Confederacy.

General Thomas "Stonewall" Jackson was a famous Confederate. He was a close friend of Robert E. Lee. He was a hero at the Battle of Bull Run and at the Battle of Chancellorsville.

He was a fierce fighter. And he earned his nickname "Stonewall" when Union army enemies could not fight their way past him.

In 1863, Jackson was scouting his army's position. He was accidentally shot by his fellow Confederate soldiers. After eight days, he died of his wounds.

General Nathan B. Forrest was bold. His unit won battle after battle in the early days of the Civil War. He became famous for leading his men on raids against the Union.

He was asked about the secret of his success. He replied, "To git thar fustest with the mostest men."

In April 1864, his troops captured and killed more than 300 former slaves. Forrest's men were defeated at Selma, Alabama, in 1865.

General Pierre G. Beauregard led the attack upon Fort Sumter. He also fought in the Battle of Bull Run in 1861. And he shared command in the Battle of Shiloh. He fought brilliantly at the Battle of Petersburg in Virginia in 1864.

General James Ewell Brown "Jeb" Stuart was a brave Confederate cavalryman. The men in the cavalry rode horses. He served with Stonewall Jackson at Bull Run and at Chancellorsville. Stuart was known for leading his men on daring rides around the enemy camps.

At Gettysburg, he decided to try one of these bold moves. But he could not get back. With Stuart away, General Lee did not have the information he needed about enemy positions. Many said it was Stuart's fault that the South lost that battle. But General Lee took the blame.

Union Leaders

General Ulysses S. Grant commanded the Union armies at the close of the Civil War. Though almost 40 years old when the Civil War began, Grant fought hard and made quick decisions.

In 1862, he and his men held off the Confederate army at Shiloh. His brave stand at Vicksburg led to the Confederate retreat there. He next fought at Chattanooga. And he led the attack against Richmond. This battle led to the defeat of the Confederate army.

General William T. Sherman served in the Battle of Bull Run. And he served with General Grant in the Battle of Shiloh. A fierce fighter, he took part in the capture of Vicksburg. And he helped rescue Grant's weakened army at Chattanooga, Tennessee.

In 1864, Sherman led 100,000 men against Atlanta, Georgia. Then he moved on to Savannah. He marched toward the Carolinas. And he ordered his men to destroy all crops, to kill the farm animals, and to blow up railroad bridges.

General Philip H. Sheridan was active in the Battle of Chattanooga. He went on to attack General Lee's troops in the Shenandoah Valley.

He also drove Southerners from their homes.

General George B. McClellan has been called the war's greatest Northern general. He led his men into many battles. And he drove back the Confederate troops many times. McClellan's forces won at the Battle of Antietam. This was the bloodiest one-day battle of the war.

In 1862, President Lincoln was unhappy. McClellan had not followed the retreating troops. And Lincoln felt McClellan was too slow to make decisions. So he replaced him.

General George Gordon Meade led troops at Bull Run, Antietam, and Chancellorsville. In 1863, he was sent to lead the North's forces at Gettysburg. When General Grant became supreme Union commander in 1864, he gave Meade the important job of Commander of the Army of the Potomac.

Sojourner Truth: Freedom Leader

Sojourner looked up at the kind face of the tall, lanky man. From her side came the voice of her friend Lucy Colman—
"President Lincoln, may I present Mrs. Sojourner Truth."
President Lincoln bowed and shook Sojourner's hand.
"I'm pleased to meet you," he said. "I've heard about your many speeches."
The president's hand is hard and rough like mine, Sojourner thought. Here is a man who knows hard work.
"You are a great man to my people," she said. "I cried with happiness when you signed the Emancipation Proclamation."
She could hardly believe she was in the White House. Sojourner thought back. It had been a long road. She had started out with nothing. She had started out as a slave.

Life as a Slave

As a child, she was called Belle Hardenburgh. But even that name was not really hers. For slave children had no last names of their own. They took the name of the family that owned them.

In Belle's case, a Dutch family, the Hardenburghs, owned her. They moved to New York in the 1790s.

Belle had 11 brothers and sisters. But she had known only one brother, Peter. All her older brothers and sisters had been sold when they were very young.

When she was 12, she had to stand on the small platform called an *auction block.* Her mother had no way to save her. But her mother said, "When you are afraid, talk to God."

On the auction block, Belle knew little of what was happening around her. She spoke only Dutch. In just a few minutes, she belonged to a man named Mr. Neely. Soon she found herself walking down the road behind his wagon.

The Neelys beat her often. Her next owners were kind. But a need for money forced them to sell her. And her new owner, Mr. Dumont, was the meanest yet. Whip marks soon covered Belle's back and arms.

When she was in her late teens, Mr. Dumont forced her to marry another slave. His name was Tom. And he was much older than Belle.

Belle continued to work hard in the fields. In time, she had five children. There were four daughters and one son.

The marriage was not a happy one. But Belle loved her children deeply.

Freedom Comes to Some

Something was happening. And New York's slaves knew little about it. In 1817, the state had passed a new law. It said that on July 4, 1827, all adult slaves in the state were to be

30

freed. Their children must work for their masters until the girls were 25 and the boys were 28. Then they would be free too.

Like many former slaves, Tom had no skills to earn a living. So Belle began working for white families. She cleaned their houses.

She had a chance to move to New York City. And Tom stayed behind. He later died in poverty.

Years went by. And Belle worked hard as a housekeeper. She often remembered her mother's words.

One night in 1843 she prayed, "Tell me what you want me to do, oh Lord. I see so many poor people around me. Even poorer than I am."

A feeling came over her. She felt that it was her duty to help other black people. She packed her clothes in a pillowcase. And she began to walk. She didn't know where she would go. But she knew she would be safe.

A New Life, a New Name

In New York and Massachusetts, white people set up outdoor churches. Belle began speaking to these groups. She walked from meeting to meeting.

That's what I am, she thought. I'm a *sojourner,* a person who walks from place to place. That will be my new name. I will spread the truth about slavery.

Then she picked "Truth" as the rest of her name.

Sojourner found other people who were against slavery. They

were called *abolitionists.* They demanded an end to slavery.

Many Americans hated abolitionists. Plantation owners in the South wanted them silenced.

Olive Gilbert asked to write Truth's story. The abolitionists sold the book at their meetings.

A few years later, Truth met Harriet Beecher Stowe, the author of *Uncle Tom's Cabin.* Many Northerners who'd read it had turned against slavery.

Mrs. Stowe so admired Sojourner Truth's work that she wrote an article about her. It appeared in *The Atlantic Monthly,* an important magazine.

The article made Sojourner Truth famous in the U.S. and even in parts of Europe.

The Price of Freedom

At age 67, Truth met President Lincoln. His Emancipation Proclamation had freed Southern slaves in 1863.

But freedom had a price. Within a year, 13,000 homeless blacks had walked to Washington, D.C., from the South. They

had no jobs and no money. Few of them could read or write.

Sojourner Truth wanted to help. A camp was set up on the banks of the Potomac River. It was called Freedmen's Village. Life was a bit better there. There was shelter. And there was hope.

"Your children must go to school and learn to read," Truth told the families. "You women who worked in the fields must now learn to cook and clean. You should know how to take care of the sick. Your families need you."

She trusted President Lincoln to help. The war was ending. So he would have more time to make a plan.

Then everything went wrong. Six days after the end of the Civil War, the president was shot and killed.

Truth had never been so sad. Even as a slave, the future had not looked this dark.

The Good Fight

Vice President Andrew Johnson became president. And Truth traveled to the White House. President Johnson was polite. And he listened carefully. But he made no promises.

Things were not improving for the former slaves in Washington, D.C. Most were willing to work. But they had no land. Farming was all they knew.

Then Truth had an idea. The U.S. still owned great areas of land in the West. Why couldn't some of that be given to the former slaves? With the right tools, they could get a new start.

She wrote letters to Congress. So did her friends. She asked people to sign pleas, or *petitions*. The petitions asked Congress to help.

Hundreds signed. And all the petitions were sent to Washington, D.C.

For four years, she traveled and spoke to the people. But Congress never took action to give up the land. At last, she became tired and ill.

In 1883, she was too sick to continue her work. She died at 86. Her daughters were at her side.

Sojourner Truth had not finished all she wanted to do. But she had tried her best. This poor slave girl had traveled the country. She had spoken the truth. She had met two presidents.

And she had left her mark on history.

Chapter 6

The Battle of Gettysburg

On July 1, 1861, John Burns heard the sound of gunfire. It was nearby.

The 72-year-old Pennsylvania shoemaker hurried to his front porch. Union soldiers were rushing past the house. They seemed ready for battle. And they were headed west toward the McPherson farm.

John Burns went inside. With a grim smile, he took down his old musket.

"They won't turn me down a third time," he vowed. "They said I was too old to enlist in 1861. And they said the same thing in '62."

The aging Scotsman ran a hand through his white hair. He rested his musket on his shoulder.

"Gettysburg is my town. And I'm going to fight for it."

A three-day struggle followed. It has been called the greatest battle ever fought on American soil.

Burns followed the Union soldiers. He hurried down the road. And he walked past Gettysburg's Lutheran Seminary. The sound of gunfire grew louder.

He soon came upon a line of men in blue. They were soldiers of the 150th Pennsylvania Volunteers.

The surprised men welcomed him with smiles. No one asked his age. The soldiers talked Burns into trading his old

musket for a newer weapon.

Burns watched as the men filled their pockets with bullets.
Then he did the same.

"Those rebels will divide our country," he said. "They'll
learn their lesson. Right here at Gettysburg."

Quickly, Burns pushed his way to the front line. His eyes
gleaming, he fired away. Years of hunting had given him a
sharp aim. He did as well as the younger men around him.

Early that afternoon, Burns received his first wound. He
stopped long enough to have it bandaged.

Now the Union forces were being driven back. They
needed him. So Burns went to the front line again. This time,
he joined a trained army unit. It was called the Iron Brigade.

He received two more flesh wounds. Then a call to
withdraw, or *retreat,* ended his fighting for that day.

That evening, the Union troops retreated through the
streets of Gettysburg. Many men were captured by the
Confederate forces.

General Meade was the commander of the Union forces.
He gathered his remaining men on Cemetery Hill. This was

south of town. Earlier in the day, the men had fought among the tombstones there.

The first day at Gettysburg was a tragic one. The Union had 12,000 dead and wounded. The Confederacy had 8,000.

That night, cries of the wounded filled the air. Union soldiers with bullet wounds staggered through town. They were thirsty and in pain.

Gettysburg citizens crept out of their homes with pitchers of water. Many families took men in. Others set up hospitals in the town's churches and warehouses.

Local and military doctors were kept busy removing bullets. They were often forced to cut off an arm or leg.

The Confederate forces took over Gettysburg on July 2. But John Burns was not arrested. For he was not a Union soldier.

Not one of Gettysburg's citizens was harmed by the Confederates. The 2,400 townspeople stayed in their houses. They were afraid of what might happen next.

Many families took food and bedding into their cellars. This offered at least some protection from the bullets and cannon balls.

Confederate officers knocked on doors. They ordered the people of Gettysburg to take in wounded rebel soldiers. Some houses were filled with bleeding men from both sides.

Mothers soon learned that these young men were much like their own sons. Some women told neighbors about how strange dinnertime had been that second night. At their tables might have been three or four injured Union soldiers. And they'd be eating alongside three or four Confederate soldiers.

All were weak with pain. So there was no fighting. As one Gettysburg mother put it—

"It could have been a family reunion. And these boys might have been cousins."

By July 3, additional troops had come to the aid of General Meade's forces. This larger army began to drive the Confederates back.

At one point, 12,000 Southern troops tried to break through the Union line. In that battle—Pickett's Charge—the Northern troops held firm. More than 5,000 young men died there. All died in just one hour.

The Southern forces could no longer continue the battle. On the morning of July 4, General Lee withdrew his men into Virginia.

The two armies finally marched away from Gettysburg. And they left behind a town in ruins.

Many homes had more than 100 bullet holes in them. Some had been burned. More than 51,000 killed and wounded soldiers were left behind. Men who needed care were crowded into every building in town. There were only a few doctors.

The men and women of Gettysburg went to work. They found papers on many bodies. These papers told each soldier's hometown.

Women and girls wrote letters to the soldiers' families. John Burns and the other men and boys buried hundreds of dead horses and cattle. The terrible smell of death was everywhere.

Pennsylvania's governor was Andrew Curtin. He set aside a large piece of land for a cemetery. Within four months, all the dead were buried. And the graves were properly marked.

On November 19, 1863, the new cemetery was dedicated. The main speaker was Edward Everett. He gave a two-hour talk.

Next came President Lincoln. He said only 270 words. His speech is known as the Gettysburg Address.

His speech lasted three minutes. But the power of his words will remain with Americans forever.

Chapter 7

Tools of War

Many advances in the weapons and methods of war were made during the Civil War. Some were successful. Others were not. The most popular advancement came with the guns used.

Rifles

Both Confederate and Union soldiers used many different types of rifles. One of the most common was the Springfield rifle. It was made in Massachusetts. It weighed nine pounds. And it was nearly five feet long.

To load his rifle, a soldier took out a paper-wrapped package. It held gunpowder. He also grabbed a bullet from a pouch hanging from his belt.

He bit off the end of the bullet. And he poured powder down the barrel. Then he pushed the bullet into the barrel. He used a long metal stick. It was called a *ramrod*. With practice, a man could load and fire three times in a minute!

In later battles, the Springfield rifle was replaced by *breech-loading* rifles. A soldier could load it from the side. So he could remain hidden on the ground rather than having to stand up.

Most Union soldiers received breech-loading weapons. But few were given to the Confederate troops. This difference was a big advantage for the Northern army.

Cannons

Most Civil War cannons were old. Firing them was dangerous. When the cannon was fired, it would *recoil,* or jump back. Sometimes it recoiled several feet.

Then men would have to roll it back into position. They'd swab out the inside and reload it.

Cannons could do much damage to the

enemy. So troops always tried to capture enemy cannons.

Cannon barrels were made from iron or bronze. The Civil War versions of the barrels had spiral grooves. These barrels sent shells spinning forward in a long, flat arc. These newer weapons were prized on the battlefield.

Ironclad Ships

When the war began, Union ships closed off the whole coast of the Confederacy. This was called a *blockade.* They wanted to keep military supplies and food from reaching the Southern states.

As the war continued, both sides built many ships. But the Confederacy never quite overcame the effects of the blockade.

In 1862, Southern forces raised a large Union ship from where it had sunk. It was the *Merrimac*. They covered it with sheets of metal. This made it an *ironclad* ship.

The *Merrimac* destroyed two of the Union's finest wooden ships. And this was in its first fight!

But the U.S. government had built its own ironclad warship. It was named the *Monitor*. It was small. And it was shaped like a drum. It moved low in the water.

The *Monitor* had a revolving gun holder. The ship turned easily. And the guns could change their aim in just a few seconds.

On March 9, 1862, the two ships met in battle. They fought for five hours. Both suffered damage.

Finally, the *Merrimac* sailed away. It sent one last shot over the top of the *Monitor*.

No one has ever decided who won the battle that day. Most call it a tie.

On the Battlefield

The Civil War was the first time that soldiers used *dugouts* and *trenches*. These are simply holes dug in the ground. They gave soldiers some protection during battle.

Black men volunteered to fight for the Union. At first, they were not allowed guns. Instead they often dug trenches for the white soldiers.

If a soldier could crawl into a trench, he might be

41

protected from a *hand grenade.* This was a chemical hand bomb. It had been tested a few times in other wars.

Grenades helped defeat the Confederacy at Vicksburg in 1863.

Some battles took thousands of lives. Each army lost about 25 out of every 100 men in a battle. At Gettysburg, the number was as high as 80 out of 100!

A soldier wanted to be sure his family knew of his fate. So he was likely to write his name and address on a handkerchief or piece of paper. Then he pinned it to his uniform before going into battle.

The use of military *dog tags,* or metal identification necklaces, is now common. Sometimes soldiers are badly wounded. And they can't answer questions about themselves. So dog tags contain the basic information.

The Camel Express?

The Confederacy had trouble moving the mail. Jefferson Davis remembered his "camel project." He'd conducted it for President Franklin Pierce in 1853. He had used camels to transport supplies to the West. And he knew there were still trained camels they could use.

So he sent some cowboys to round up the animals.

From 1863 to 1865, a few camels were used to move the Confederate mail. Most of this was done in the western states. The animals were hard to train. And the noise of war bothered them. So they became hard to handle.

After the war, the federal government sold the animals to circuses. Some were turned loose on the desert. Some of those were hunted by the Apache Indians.

Other camels disappeared into the hills. Even in the 1900s, their offspring were sometimes seen in California's Death Valley.

Chapter 8

Children in the Ranks

Boys as young as 16 or 17 fought for both armies. Sadly, these boys were often the first killed in action. It was because they'd been poorly trained, and they were too young to fully understand the dangers.

But there was an even younger group of boys. Some were as young as nine or ten. They were the drummer boys.

A drummer boy woke the troops at dawn. He led practice marches. And he even led men into battle. He often worked with another young man who played a fife. Sometimes yet another young boy played the bugle.

These boys marched in front of the troops. But they carried no weapons.

An officer always kept his drummer boy close at hand. Sometimes things did not go well. And the army had to fall back. The drummer's rat-a-tat gave the command.

Or perhaps a drummer boy would beat his drumsticks. That was the signal to charge ahead.

These boys joined the armies in great numbers. Thousands served in the Civil War.

Drummer boys and fifers had other duties too. These were jobs that made them grow up very quickly.

In the thick of battle, these boys took care of the injured. As soon as a soldier fell, the drummer boys reached for a stretcher. And they carried him back behind the lines to be treated.

A lad soon learned to tend to a man who was shot in the chest. Or he learned to help a soldier whose arm or leg had been blown off. Childhood seemed far behind. War was very real.

Two drummer boys have become more famous than the rest.

Johnny Clem was a nine-year-old from Ohio. His nickname was "The Drummer Boy of Chickamauga." He fought bravely for the entire four years of the Civil War.

Later, he stayed in the army. He served a total of 55 years in uniform.

Willie Johnston was an 11-year-old from Vermont. He served so well that he was noticed by President Lincoln.

In September of 1863, Willie received the Congressional Medal of Honor. He was the seventh soldier ever to receive the award. And he remains the youngest so honored.

No one doubts that these young heroes showed tremendous bravery.

Chapter 9

A Letter from Prison

The Civil War lasted four years. Each side took about 200,000 prisoners. One in every seven died before they could be released.

Old factories and warehouses became prisons. When those were full, men were sometimes placed in *stockades*. These were open acres of land, fenced all around.

Prisoners were expected to shelter themselves however they could. Below, a Union prisoner writes home. He's in Andersonville. That was the Confederate prison in Georgia.

June 20, 1864

My dearest Martha,

This poor excuse for a letter may never reach you. But I will take that chance. My heart is so full. I must write down what has happened these last weeks.

On May 11, I was following General Sheridan on an attack against Richmond. A bullet caught my horse in the throat. I ran into the woods. All at once, I was surrounded by rebel soldiers.

Three weeks have passed since they marched me here to Andersonville. It is an open space with guarded fences all around. Some say there are 30,000 men here. It is very crowded. And the prison is filthy.

The Georgia sun beats down on us. No trees of any kind give us shade. And we have no roof over our heads unless we can find a way to build a shelter ourselves.

Our water comes from a stream. It is no wider across than I

am tall. And it is about ankle-deep. Before it reaches us, the stream passes through the guards' camp. By the time it gets here, it is dark in color. And it gives off a terrible smell.

Since we have no other water, we drink and cook from the stream. I am learning to strain, or *filter*, it as best I can. I found a torn piece of burlap from a prisoner who died last week. I strain the water through that.

The camp cookhouse is next to the stream. That adds rotting food and grease to the already foul water. Should I wonder, dear Martha, that so many men here suffer from fever?

We have little shelter from the hot June sun. But we can stretch coats and scraps of blankets over ourselves. The rain cools us some. We are glad for thunderstorms. For then we wash ourselves and our clothes.

A few men have made low mud houses from the dirty water and clay soil. An army buddy, James, had agreed to build

such a hut with me. We made our plan last night. But when I awoke this morning, he lay on the ground beside me. Dead. I will try to find another man to build with.

Each evening, we are given our rations for all of the next day. We get a square of cornbread. It is made with the cob ground in with the kernels.

The other men have taught me to pick out the weevils. A few men just leave them in. They have come to like the taste.

Some days, we have a small piece of salted pork too. And about twice a week, two tablespoons of rice. A man next to me says we receive two tablespoons of molasses each month. But I have not seen that happen.

The men around me are thin as skeletons. Nearly half have no clothes at all. I think I might stay alive on the food given to me. However, the fear I have is of illness. Food will not keep me alive if it comes back up.

Dozens around me stare into space. Or just lie about the ground. Men die here at the rate of 75 a day.

We must all watch out for each other. So I spend much time trying to cheer the weakest men. In the morning, each group of 90 must line up for roll call. If a man is missing, his group will receive no rations that day.

I am sorry to bring all this sad news to you, Martha. But it helps to write this letter. Remembering our life in New York is what keeps me going.

There is one sure way out of the pain and suffering here. It is one I pray I will not be driven to take.

I told you there were no trees in the stockade. Here is the reason. They were cut down to make a fence out of the upright trunks. I judge it to be about 20 feet high. Near the top are small platforms. The guards sit there with their rifles.

About 20 feet inside that high fence is a smaller one. It runs parallel to it. This smaller fence is known as the "dead line." You might put a foot or finger over that inside fence. But

it will be blown away by a flurry of bullets from the guards.

By now, dear Martha, I think you've guessed what I meant by "a way out of the misery." Just yesterday, I saw a man hobble to the inner fence. He looked to see if the guard was watching. When he knew he had been seen, he moved forward.

Taking his last bit of energy, he climbed over the inner fence. In an instant, the guards filled his body with bullets. Clearly, that man wanted to escape Andersonville. In the only way he could.

I promise not to do something so foolish, dear Martha. Though the days ahead may be difficult, I will do all I can to go on. I pray this war will end. And while I am still strong enough to find my way back to New York. I long to hold you and the children.

I ask your prayers.

Your loving husband,
Nathan

Chapter **10**

War's End

Hard Times in the South

After the Battle of Gettysburg, things looked grim for the South. The Confederate army began losing most of its battles. And Union troops pushed farther into the South.

It had been two years. And Confederate President Jefferson Davis saw that England would not help the South.

Union blockades kept food and supplies from southern ports. And farm machinery broke down often. These farm tools had been made in northern factories. So no spare parts could be found.

There had been food shortages for more than a year. Southern farmers had long ago stopped growing cotton and tobacco. They now planted only things people could eat.

But it was difficult to move the food to the cities. Railroads and waterways had been captured or damaged. Everyone was hungry.

Coffee and sugar were scarce. There was no salt to preserve meat. Beef and dairy cattle, pigs, and chickens disappeared from farmyards.

In Richmond, a bread riot broke out. Hungry, angry women smashed windows. They fired pistols and raided stores. President Davis tried to calm the rioters. He told them to blame the United States for their problems.

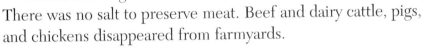

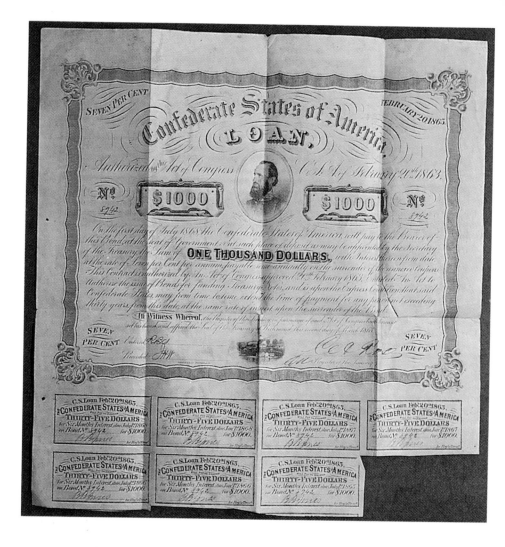

Confederate soldiers worried about the hard life their families were leading. In the final years of the war, 200,000 of them left, or *deserted*. All they could think of was returning home to help.

The Confederate government began printing large amounts of paper money. And the value of a dollar went down. Then it took several dollars to buy what had earlier cost just one.

In 1863, it took $3,400 Confederate dollars to buy what had cost $120 at the beginning of the war! Flour prices went from $200 to $1,100 a barrel. Bacon prices rose from $2 to $20.

The Battle Was Lost

Edmund Ruffin

Edmund Ruffin was a fiery rebel soldier. He had fired one of the first shots on Fort Sumter.

In 1865, he could not accept the South's defeat. So he wrapped himself in a Confederate flag. And he killed himself with a bullet to the head.

General J. O. Shelby

Confederate General J. O. Shelby vowed not to lay down his weapons. He headed for Mexico at the end of the war. Three other generals and the governors of Texas and Louisiana went with him.

Following behind them came 1,000 of Shelby's cavalrymen. This group later scattered throughout Mexico, Cuba, and Brazil.

The Death of a President

President Lincoln was in Richmond when the war ended. He heard of the meeting at Appomattox Courthouse. And he returned to Washington, D.C. He had to make plans for peace. How he longed to bring the nation together again!

A few days later, the president attended a play. It was being performed at Ford's Theater.

SURRAT. BOOTH. HAROLD.

War Department, Washington, April 20, 1865,

☞ **$100,000 REWARD!**

THE MURDERER

Of our late beloved President, Abraham Lincoln,

IS STILL AT LARGE.

$50,000 REWARD

Will be paid by this Department for his apprehension, in addition to any reward offered by Municipal Authorities or State Executives.

$25,000 REWARD

Will be paid for the apprehension of JOHN H. SURRATT, one of Booth's Accomplices.

$25,000 REWARD

Will be paid for the apprehension of David C. Harold, another of Booth's accomplices.

LIBERAL REWARDS will be paid for any information that shall conduce to the arrest of either of the above-named criminals, or their accomplices.

All persons harboring or secreting the said persons, or either of them, or aiding or assisting their concealment or escape, will be treated as accomplices in the murder of the President and the attempted assassination of the Secretary of State, and shall be subject to trial before a Military Commission and the punishment of DEATH.

Let the stain of innocent blood be removed from the land by the arrest and punishment of the murderers.

All good citizens are exhorted to aid public justice on this occasion. Every man should consider his own conscience charged with this solemn duty, and rest neither night nor day until it be accomplished.

EDWIN M. STANTON, Secretary of War.

DESCRIPTIONS.—BOOTH is Five Feet 7 or 8 inches high, slender build, high forehead, black hair, black eyes, and wears a heavy black moustache.

JOHN H. SURRAT is about 5 feet, 9 inches. Hair rather thin and dark; eyes rather light; no beard. Would weigh 145 or 150 pounds. Complexion rather pale and clear, with color in his cheeks. Wore light clothes of fine quality. Shoulders square; cheek bones rather prominent; chin narrow; ears projecting at the top; forehead rather low and square, but broad. Parts his hair on the right side; neck rather long. His lips are firmly set. A slim man.

DAVID C. HAROLD is five feet six inches high, hair dark, eyes dark, eyebrows rather heavy, full face, nose short, hand short and fleshy, feet small, instep high, round bodied, naturally quick and active, slightly closes his eyes when looking at a person.

NOTICE.—In addition to the above, State and other authorities have offered rewards amounting to almost one hundred thousand dollars, making an aggregate of about **TWO HUNDRED THOUSAND DOLLARS.**

Suddenly, John Wilkes Booth entered the president's box. Booth was an actor who hated the North.

Booth shot Lincoln in the head. The president died the next morning.

Many of Lincoln's dreams had come true. The Civil War restored the United States of America. It also ended slavery.

In 1865, the 13th Amendment to the U.S. Constitution was passed. It abolished slavery forever. No longer could one man own another.

America's saddest war was over.